Kenneth M Weigel

Ski the Champion's Way

THE CHAMPION'S WAY

by Ernie McCulloch

HARPER & ROW, PUBLISHERS, New York, Evanston, and London

SKI THE CHAMPION'S WAY. Copyright © 1967 by Universal Publishing & Distributing Corp. Printed in the United States of America. All rights reserved. No part of this book may be used or reproduced in any manner whatsoever without written permission except in the case of brief quotations embodied in critical articles and reviews. For information address Harper & Row, Publishers, Incorporated, 49 East 33rd Street, New York, N.Y. 10016.

LIBRARY OF CONGRESS CATALOG CARD NUMBER: 67-22546

A-T

CONTENTS

Preface   ix

Introduction   xi

BEGINNING SKIING

Carrying Skis and Poles   2
Walking on Skis   4
Climbing: Side Step   6
Climbing: Diagonal Side Step   8
Climbing: Herringbone   10
Straight Running   12
Kick Turn   14
Snowplow   16
Snowplow Turn   18
Linked Snowplow Turns   20

INTERMEDIATE SKIING

Traversing   24
Single Stemming   26
Snowplow-Turn Exercise   28
Snowplow Turn with Traverse   30
Sideslipping   32
Sideslipping Forward   34
Sideslip Traverse Exercise   36
Christie-into-the-Hill with Down-Unweighting   38
Christie-into-the-Hill with Up-Unweighting   40
Snowplow Weight-Transfer Exercise   42
Snowplow Christie   44
Uphill Stem Christie   46

PARALLEL SKIING

Down-and-Up Pole Exercise   52
Hop Between Poles   54
Hop Down the Fall Line   56
Transition to Parallel Skiing   58
Fall-Line Parallel Skiing   60
Pole Action   64

ADVANCED SKIING

Long Parallel Turn Without Edge Set   68
Edge Set and Pole Action   70
Edge Set Starting a Parallel Turn   72
Edge Set and a Complete Parallel Turn   74
Linked Sharp Turns with Edge Set   76
Narrow Edge-Set Turns   78
Edge Set on a Very Steep Hill   80
Edge Set Using Both Poles on an Extremely Steep Slope   82
Jump Christie   84
Jump Christie in Deep Snow   86
Parallel Turns in Deep Snow   88

JUMPING AND TRICK SKIING

Riding Small, Sharp Bumps   96
Prejumping Small Bumps   100
Prejumping a Small Bump and Jumping a Large Bump   102
Jumping a Series of Bumps   104
Airplane Turn   108
Jump Turn with Both Poles   110
Geländesprung, or Double Pole-Jump Turn   112
360-Degree Turnaround from a Stop Christie   114
One-Ski Skiing   116

COMPETITIVE SKIING

Skate Turn with Tip Pull   120
Skate Turn Without Tip Pull   122
Slalom   124
Side-Hill Hairpin and Open Gate   126
Four Closed Gates   128
Closed Off-Set Gates: Comparison Runs   132
Straight Flush   138
Straight Flush: Comparison Runs   142
Giant Slalom   144
Downhill Crouches   146

PREFACE

Except, possibly, for a few self-taught hermits in the Tibetan Mountains, just about every skier who ever hit the slopes has heard of Ernie McCulloch—if not for his racing achievements, then for his outstanding ski teaching. Here is a man who has literally lived skiing since he was four years old, when he began following his brother's cross-country ski tracks around Three Rivers, Quebec.

Fortunately, Ernie's skiing excellence doesn't stop when the snow melts into puddles. In fact, one aspect of his ski talent—writing—begins then. Every year since 1958, when *Ski Life Magazine* started, and on through its incorporation with *Ski Magazine,* Ernie has been a technical editor and a major contributor of teaching articles. His clear, concise words accompanied by precise demonstrations have done much to clarify the often vague language and methods of ski teaching lore. Moreover, his first book, *Learn to Ski,* was printed in two editions and is probably the all-time best-selling ski instruction book.

This kind of excellence is the same ingredient that made Ernie a champion racer. It all started when Ernie was a teen-age ski jumper and the winner of about every meet in the Laurentians. One day in 1947, for variety, he entered an Alpine racing event and placed second behind a skier who was considered "the" hot young racer. Ernie immediately switched to Alpine competition. In fact, he left the technical school he was attending and started a lifetime career in skiing, first on the ski patrol at Mont Tremblant and, after passing a course given by the Canadian Ski Instructors' Alliance, as a ski instructor. Being on skis every day gave him a chance to train hard, for a while under the direction of Emille Allais, the famous French coach. By 1949, Ernie had won everything in the Laurentians and, after beating the French Olympic Team in the Quebec-Kandahar, decided to go to the Western meets. A missed gate disqualified him from the Harriman Cup at Sun Valley, but his over-all performance earned him a job as racing-class coach at the Sun Valley Ski School.

Continuing to race the following year, Ernie won the National Giant Slalom, the North American Championships, the National

Downhill Championships, and the Harriman Cup—and the title Grand Slam Champion. The next year saw more wins on the McCulloch record (beating such famous names as Othmar Schneider and Stein Eriksen) and another accolade from a poll of sports writers as Skier of the Half-Century.

During this period, he was asked to head the ski school at Mont Tremblant Lodge. Seeing an opportunity not only to return to his beloved Laurentians, but also to put some of his imaginative teaching ideas into practice, he accepted. With vast experience and great energy he built one of the best ski schools in the world while helping to establish Mont Tremblant as an outstanding ski resort.

As his reputation as a ski teacher spread, Ernie has spent more and more of his time refining the art. He was president of the Canadian Ski Instructors' Alliance for two years, chief examiner for three years, and, most recently, chief demonstrator and coach of the Canadian Interski Team that performs at the World Congress of Ski Instructors.

Never too far from racing, however, Ernie has coached Canadian Olympic and F.I.S. teams and spends the months of June and July coaching youngsters at a summer racing school at Mount Hood, Oregon.

Racer, teacher, coach—Ernie McCulloch deserves his reputation as one of the most knowledgeable men in the ski world. His regular "Ski Clinic" column in *Ski Magazine* draws scores of letters each month seeking advice on every conceivable aspect of the sport, and Ernie is never stopped for an answer.

In this book Ernie again concentrates his teaching talent, his long experience, and his imaginative approach to produce one of the best ski instruction books written to date. His sincerity and devotion toward helping you become a better skier are reflected on every page.

ARNOLD E. ABRAMSON
President and Publisher
Ski Magazine

INTRODUCTION

There has been tremendous progress in the world of skiing during the past ten years. Equipment has improved enormously. The pair of boots you can purchase in almost any ski shop today is as good as—if not better than—a pair that would have been purchased by a champion competitor a decade ago. The construction of skis has become more and more of a science, and ski manufacturers everywhere are competing to improve such things as flex, holding qualities, the matching of pairs, running surfaces, edges, finish of both tops and side walls, and heel and toe protectors. The skier of today can purchase equipment that is consistently of high quality and which makes skiing much easier than it was in the past.

Teaching has also come a long way, because of better training of instructors, competition among a growing number of ski schools, and meetings of professionals at conventions and congresses to discuss the best facets of different techniques and to pool experience and knowledge.

In fact, so much has been said about technique during the past five or six years in various periodicals and books that I believe a lot of skiers have become somewhat confused as to what the body should actually be doing throughout a whole ski turn. Yet, it has pretty well been proved that all top skiers today ski with very similar body mechanics, regardless of which country they come from. The greatest similarity in technique among the champion skiers is the way they all use their arms: away from the body for balance and always moving in a circular motion in the same direction as the turn. I feel that the importance of the arm position in skiing has been neglected. The arms play a very important part in maintaining balance and in helping your body to move in the direction of the turn. When a good skier is demonstrating a turn, his hips are always slightly reversed to the turn and the outside arm is always moving forward bringing his body square to his skis at the end of the turn.

In some sequences in this book I have deliberately compared two other skiers with myself to show the similarity in our body positions and arm motions. These are two well-known skiers in international competition—Pepi Stiegler, former gold medalist from Austria, and Adrien Duvillard, champion skier from France.

I have tried to make the book easy to understand by showing lots of sequence pictures and by using concise and easily understood captions. Terms that are unique to skiing are defined when they are first used in the book. I still believe that too much writing and too many detailed instructions will only confuse the reader. Special thanks for helping me maintain this simplicity of presentation go to Paul Ryan for his excellent photography and to Janet Nelson for her help in preparing the text.

The first part of the book is for the novice and intermediate and the last part for the advanced intermediate and expert. I have shown many ways to ski parallel—on flat hills, steep hills, and extremely steep hills. There are also sections on skiing over bumps, racing crouches, and slalom. I hope it will prove helpful to you in your total enjoyment of skiing.

Ernie McCulloch

Mont Tremblant, Quebec
October, 1967

BEGINNING SKIING

Carrying Skis and Poles

Here are two methods of carrying skis. Either method is satisfactory, and the one you use depends on where and how far you are carrying them.

This method is useful when carrying skis in a crowd, for short distances, and when climbing open slopes. When climbing rather steep slopes you can use your poles with one hand. Notice that the skis are strapped together in the middle.

This method is usually used when you have a long way to go. The poles help support and distribute the weight of the skis evenly on both shoulders. When skis are being carried a long distance, I recommend that they be tied together.

Walking on Skis

Walking should be practiced on flat terrain. The first time you walk on skis it helps to begin without poles. After a few steps you will find that the pole action will come automatically.

As the left foot moves forward the right arm moves ahead and the pole is planted. Keep your weight on the forward ski while you are preparing to move the other foot forward.

The right foot moves forward and the left arm moves ahead.

Climbing: Side Step

This is the easiest way for beginners to climb a slope. It is also used by all skiers when climbing a narrow, rather steep trail. Practice it first on level ground, then on gradually steeper slopes. Practice in light snow as well as on hard-packed snow, keeping both skis well edged (set at an angle so their edges bite into the snow) *at all times. Step sideways up the slope with skis perpendicular to the* fall line (*the steepest grade of the hill*).

Place skis horizontally across the slope, well edged, with feet close together.

Step uphill with the uphill ski, edging it well into the snow. Uphill pole moves up with uphill ski.

Shifting your weight to the uphill ski, bring the downhill ski up close to it. Downhill pole moves up after downhill ski.

Climbing: Diagonal Side Step

The diagonal side step is an easy and less tiring method of climbing across and up a wide slope because it combines the walking step with the side step. Each step will take you both upward and forward.

With skis horizontally across the slope, move the uphill ski forward and upward.

The uphill ski is edged well into the snow. With the weight on the uphill ski, the downhill ski is picked up and brought forward and parallel. The poles move as in walking—right leg, left pole; left leg, right pole.

Climbing: Herringbone

The herringbone is an efficient way to climb a short, steep hill. It should not be used for a climb of any length because it is tiring. Even good skiers only use it for six or seven steps, but it is very effective in its proper place. It should be practiced at first on a flat or almost flat terrain and then on a steeper slope. On steep slopes, placing your hands on top of your poles will give you more power and will be less tiring.

With skis in a "V" position, lift your right ski up and place it on its inside edge.

Transfer your weight to the right ski and, with the support of your poles, lift the left ski onto its inside edge. The poles are used as an aid moving alternately with the opposite leg. The step should be just long enough to keep the skis from crossing one another at the back.

Straight Running

Now that you've climbed up the slope you are ready to ski down. Before trying it, practice the running position on level ground until you can assume it quickly. A supple, relaxed body is the first requisite. Your weight should be evenly distributed on both skis, knees slightly flexed and hips upright. This up-and-down exercise will improve your balance. Practice it after you have done some straight running.

The only difference between the stance of a running position and your normal standing position is a slight flex in the knees. Arms are curved slightly with hands forward and low. Points of poles are to the rear.

From a straight running position, lower your body into a semi-crouch position. Then, raise your body to resume the straight running position. Repeat this rhythmic up and down movement as you travel down the slope.

Kick Turn

The kick turn is a common method used to change direction. This turn should be practiced on the flat before it is attempted on the slope. It is a good idea to swing your ski up on its heel a few times for balance before attempting to do this turn.

With hands on top of the poles place the uphill pole in the snow at the tip of the skis and the downhill pole close to the rear of the skis.

With all weight on the uphill ski, kick the downhill ski forward and up on its heel. Support your balance with poles and arms.

Keeping its tail on the snow, swing the tip of the downhill ski around and down parallel to the uphill ski but pointing in the opposite direction.

Shift your weight to the downhill ski while bringing the unweighted ski around and parallel. The uphill pole follows.

Snowplow

There are two important reasons why I believe the snowplow should be taught and why it is still used in most techniques today. First, it gives a novice a feeling of security because he knows he can control his speed. This, of course, builds up confidence. Secondly, from this position it is easier to help the beginner to understand the body mechanics of skiing. The body movements in a snowplow turn are very similar to those used in christie turns. I do not believe that a skier should become dependent on the snowplow or on the single snowplow turn. Just as soon as he is ready to change direction he should move on to experience the thrill of linking snowplow turns down the slope. You should never try to do snowplow turns on too steep a hill. Practice on a gentle slope with a flat top and a level outrun.

Tails of the skis are apart. Tips are close together but not touching. Skis are edged slightly inward. The knees are slightly flexed and the body is centered over the skis with weight evenly distributed as in the straight running position.

To increase the braking effect, the width of the plow and the edging should be increased, as in this picture.

Snowplow Turn

This is a very simple turn to execute once you have mastered the straight snowplow. Keep in mind that a ski is designed to turn easily. When one ski carries more weight than the other, it will respond and want to turn for you. It is important to remember to maintain a proper snowplow position throughout the entire maneuver.

Start down the hill in a straight snowplow position. After you descend a few feet, the right arm and shoulder are moved slightly back. The upper body now tilts to the outside, and the weight is transferred to the right ski.

The right knee is suddenly flexed and the turning power is increased. Simultaneously the *outside arm* (the arm on the outside of the arc of the turn) begins moving forward in the same direction as the turn.

At the end of the turn the body is *square* to the skis (the shoulders are at right angles to the skis) and in a position for a turn in the other direction.

Linked Snowplow Turns

It is easy to execute a series of snowplow turns after you have practiced the turn in each direction.

1. At the start of the turn the body is square to the skis. Then, the uphill arm and shoulder move slightly to the rear and the body tilts to the outside.

3. At the end of the turn the body is again square to the skis. Notice how the knees are well flexed and the upper body is leaning slightly forward.

2. The downhill knee flexes suddenly, increasing the weight on the downhill ski. At this point the outside arm is moving forward.

INTERMEDIATE SKIING

Traversing

*A proper traverse position is very important because a good many of the advanced turns start from a traverse. The essential points to remember are to have most of your weight on the downhill ski and to keep the uphill ski far enough ahead to prevent the skis from crossing. To keep the weight mainly on the downhill ski, the knees should be pressed together and into the hill with the upper body tilted slightly downhill (*this is the *angulated* position*). The uphill shoulder leads with the downhill shoulder slightly back and lower. The uphill ski is always slightly advanced.*

A front view of a traverse position on a fairly steep hill. Notice the position of the knees tilted toward the slope in relation to the upper body. This is angulation. The downhill shoulder is slightly lower and the arms are held away from the body.

Side view of a traverse position on a somewhat flatter slope. Notice that the knees are not tilted in as much as in picture 1 and that there is less angulation of the upper body. The arms are held in the same manner and the downhill shoulder is again dropped slightly. Angulation should not be exaggerated when traversing flat or moderate terrain.

Single Stemming

Single stemming is very important to learn at this point because from now on a good many of your turns will be started by stemming *the uphill ski (moving the tail of one ski so the skis form a "V") and* counterrotating *(turning your shoulders in the direction opposite to the turn). Practice this exercise on a wide slope if possible so that it can be repeated.*

Start in a traverse position.

With the weight on the downhill ski, step the uphill ski into a half-snowplow position. At the same time, move the uphill arm back and the downhill arm forward. This is called counterrotation.

Step the stemmed ski back parallel to the downhill ski. As you are stepping, the body starts to unwind back to the traverse position. Resume the traverse position.

Snowplow-Turn Exercise

This exercise will help you to perform correct body movements throughout the turn. Without your poles, extend your arms straight out from your shoulders. As your arms move with the turn, your body will automatically also turn in the proper manner.

Start in a traverse position with arms extended.

Counterrotate, allowing one arm to move backward and the other to move forward simultaneously.

Toward the completion of the turn, note the position of the arms in relation to the skis.

Snowplow Turn with Traverse

This is a good turn for a novice to use in order to ski safely down a wide slope. It is executed in exactly the same manner as the linked snowplow turn, but in between each turn the skis are brought together parallel into a traverse position.

2. Counterrotate and step the uphill ski into a stem position.

3. The body leans to the outside of the turn and the weight is transferred to the outside ski.

1. Start in a traverse position.

4. As the new direction is reached, all the weight is carried on the downhill ski.

5. The inside ski is lifted and placed parallel to the downhill ski. You are once again in the traverse position.

Sideslipping

Sideslipping should be practiced a great deal, because from now on all of your turns will be sliding turns. Before learning the christie *turns (turns in which the skis are parallel and slide sideways over the snow as the turn is completed), you must learn to sideslip—deliberately controlling the direction, speed, and duration of your slide. Mastery of sideslipping will prove extremely valuable as you progress. It will give you confidence on your skis and will help you to control your edging. Practice on well-packed snow on a short, rather steep pitch.*

In the photographs illustrating the straight sideslip, the forward sideslip, and the christie-into-the-hill exercise, you will notice that I am unweighting my skis to start them sliding by down-unweighting *(a sudden dropping of the body to release weight from the skis). I believe in using down-unweighting during the above exercises because it gives you a better understanding of the proper body position for christie turns. When a skier learns all of the sideslipping maneuvers*

Close-up shot of a sideslip position. The traverse position is maintained while sideslipping. The uphill ski is slightly advanced. The downhill shoulder is lower than the uphill shoulder.

with down-unweighting, he knows exactly what to do with his body in the last part of any christie turn—sink down. He also avoids developing the bad habit of overrotating.

From the stem christie turn on, I use up-unweighting *(a rising motion of the body to release weight from the skis) to start the turn. By that time I feel that pupils fully understand the proper body movements during the last and crucial part of the turn, which they have learned through down-unweighting in the exercises described here.*

Start by standing in a traverse position facing downhill.

The skis are unweighted by a sudden, but slight bending of the knees, and the edges of the skis are released by rolling the ankles and knees away from the hill. (It sometimes helps to start off by pushing with both poles from the uphill side.) To bring the sideslip to a stop, the skis are edged into the hill by rolling the knees and ankles in toward the hill. Regulate the speed of the sideslip by increasing or decreasing the edging of the skis.

Sideslipping Forward

Sideslipping forward will give you much the same sensation as a sliding turn. Speed should be increased as you improve. The steeper your line of descent in the traverse the more your speed will increase.

3. The momentum of the traverse and the release of the edges will start the skis sliding down and forward.

1. Start moving down the hill in a shallow traverse position.

2. The skis are unweighted by a sudden, slight lowering of the knees as the edges of the skis are released by rolling the ankles and knees outward.

Sideslip Traverse Exercise

This exercise is done in exactly the same manner as the forward sideslip just described, except that after the skis have slid for some time the knees and ankles are rolled inward. This causes the skis to edge and allows you to resume the traverse position. It is good practice in edge control.

Start in a traverse position as in the previous exercise. Then, with a slight, sudden down motion of the knees, the skis are unweighted. The ankles and knees are rolled outward and the skis begin to slide down and forward.

After sliding some distance the knees and ankles are rolled inward, causing the skis to edge, and the traverse position is resumed.

Christie-into-the-Hill with Down-Unweighting

A christie-into-the-hill is important to practice because it is actually the last half of a christie turn. It is a combination of the traverse and a forward sideslip into the hill. This is another excellent exercise for practice in edge control.

When some speed has been gained, a sudden dropping of the knees with a slight roll to the outside unweights and flattens the skis and causes them to start sliding.

As the skis begin sliding there is a continuous downward pressure of the knees and the outside arm begins slowly moving forward.

The outside arm has now moved forward and the body is almost square to the skis.

At the end of the turn the body is square or almost square to the skis. During this whole maneuver the downhill hip never moves ahead of the uphill hip. Leading with the downhill hip is a common mistake made by intermediates.

Christie-into-the-Hill with Up-Unweighting

This is exactly the same maneuver as the previous exercise, except that up-unweighting is used. In the first sequence, I have shown the way I teach with down-unweighting. In this sequence of pictures I am showing the christie-into-the-hill with up-unweighting to illustrate the difference.

Notice how pictures 2 and 3 differ from pictures 2 and 3 in the preceding sequence. In this sequence the skis are unweighted and flattened by a rise of the body from the knees, and the knees are pressed down again as the skis begin to slide.

Snowplow Weight-Transfer Exercise

This is a weight-shift exercise leading to the snowplow christie and stem christie turns. It helps your balance and teaches you to step your skis parallel from a "V" position. This exercise should be practiced on a slope that is not too steep.

Start descending the slope in a snowplow position slightly off the fall line. The upper shoulder leads slightly.

With the weight on the downhill ski, the tail of the uphill ski is picked up and stepped in parallel to the downhill ski.

When the skis are parallel the downhill shoulder is still slightly back and you are in a traverse position. Notice that there is little angulation of the body in these pictures because I am on a very flat slope. After running a few feet in the traverse position, open the skis into a snowplow position again by stepping the uphill ski out and repeat the exercise.

Snowplow Christie

The snowplow christie is another exercise leading to a stem christie. The turn begins in the fall line and ends in the same manner as the christie-into-the-hill. Practice the turn on a slope that is not too steep. It is somewhat easier if done over a very small knoll.

4. Notice the position of the body and how the outside arm is moving forward and bringing the body square or almost square to the skis.

1. Start in a narrow snowplow position with skis only slightly edged.

2. When you have gained some speed the weight is transferred to the outside ski and, with an up motion, the inside ski is picked up and brought parallel.

3. With a continuous downward pressure of the knees, the turn is completed.

Uphill Stem Christie

You are now ready to learn the stem christie, which will enable you to make swift, efficient turns in all kinds of snow. As speed increases, the angle of the stem decreases until at high speed, the skis are almost parallel. Practice this on a slope of about 15 to 20 degrees.

Start in a traverse position.

Stem the uphill ski and, at the same time, move one arm forward and the other arm back.

With a slight up-and-forward motion, the tail of the downhill ski is picked up and brought parallel to the uphill ski. ⟶

Uphill Stem Christie (continued)

With a downward motion of the knees, the tails of the skis are pushed out. The skis begin turning.

While the skis are turning, the outside arm begins moving forward.

At the end of the turn the outside arm has moved forward and the body is square to the skis and ready to start another turn.

PARALLEL SKIING

Down-and-Up Pole Exercise

In this exercise, and from now on, you will be introduced to pole action or pole planting. The reason that I have not used pole plants before this is to avoid any possibility of developing a dependency on poles. If you learn to make a good turn without planting your pole, it is easier to learn the pole plant correctly and to the best advantage in parallel turns. This exercise is a good introduction to pole action. It is extremely important to practice it on almost flat terrain with just enough slope to move your skis.

3. As your feet approach the pole, the pole is released and the body rises. The opposite arm is now brought forward and is ready to plant the pole as the body lowers once again.

1. Start in a straight running position.

2. Lower your hips and knees, bringing your right arm and pole forward. Plant the pole in the snow approximately one foot behind the tip of the ski.

53

Hop Between Poles

This exercise will give you practice in moving both skis together as well as practice in flexing your hips and knees. It will also familiarize you with retracting your skis from the snow and landing gently. The exercise is done on flat terrain from a standstill.

Start with your skis parallel and with your poles planted to the sides. The body lowers into a semi-crouch position.

With the support of your poles hop your skis off the snow and change direction slightly. (An important thing to remember when doing this exercise is not to jump the skis too far off the fall line. It is just a small hop from side to side.)

Upon landing, the skis are edged slightly and the hips and knees lower to absorb shock. This will automatically place your body in a position for another hop. The skis are again retracted, or lifted, and jumped in the opposite direction.

Hop Down the Fall Line

The down-and-up pole exercise is now combined with the previous hop exercise. This hop down the fall line is very close to fall-line parallel skiing. It should be practiced on a very flat slope in the beginning and then on a gradually steeper slope as you improve.

Start down the fall line. Lower your hips and knees and plant your left pole in the snow.

With a little hop, retract your skis and change direction slightly. During this hop the body rises and the opposite arm and pole are brought forward.

As the skis come in contact with the snow again, absorb the shock by lowering your hips and knees. At the same time the right pole is planted and you are ready to retract your skis and jump in the opposite direction.

Transition to Parallel Skiing

After you have practiced the hop down the fall line and you feel that you can do that exercise with a fair amount of rhythm, you are ready to attempt fall-line skiing with less lifting of the skis off the snow. Your speed should now be increased.

Start by making two or three hops down the fall line. As your rhythm and speed increase you will find that your skis turn automatically with less and less lifting.

Control of edging and the transfer of weight at this point is crucial. When the body rises the skis should be as flat as possible. As the skis begin to turn a bit more edging is necessary. Always remember that any time the body rises to start a turn, the skis flatten and change edges. At this point most of the weight is transferred to the outside ski.

Fall-Line Parallel Skiing

In this sequence I am skiing faster and therefore I am not using as much down-up-down motion as before. The control of my edging is more delicate—in fact, the skis are almost flat on the snow during this type of turn. Notice that the skis are never very far away from the fall line. This type of turn is effective on a hill that is not too steep. Because you will gain much too much speed on a steep slope, I definitely do not recommend it on a steep slope unless you are in the expert class.

At the end of one turn, the body lowers very slightly and the pole is planted.

The body rises from the knees and the weight is transferred to the outside ski. At the same time the outside arm moves forward. As the skis enter the fall line the body is square to the skis. (In ski teaching this position is called the *neutral position*.)

When the tails of the skis cross the fall line, there is a slight downward motion in the knees and the opposite pole is planted. ⟶

Fall-Line Parallel Skiing (continued)

At the start of the turn, notice how the outside arm again moves ahead.

Since the body is never turned very far away from the fall line, it is only slightly angulated.

Again the body rises and the outside arm moves forward.

The skis are almost flat in the fall line.

63

Pole Action

There is no set position in which the skier plants the pole or any set rule regarding the angle of the arm in relation to the body. It depends upon your speed, the sharpness of your turn, the steepness of the hill, and even upon snow conditions. All through the advanced sequences showing different types of parallel skiing you will find that my arm and pole are often in different positions, depending on the slope, speed, and type of snow.

This is a close-up showing proper arm and pole position when skiing a medium-grade slope. The arm is forward and curved, and slightly away from the body. Note the position of the pole and the arm in relation to the skis.

This picture shows the edge set and pole plant on a steep hill. Notice the difference in the angle of the arm and pole and also the difference in where the pole is planted in comparison with picture 1.

ADVANCED SKIING

Long Parallel Turn Without Edge Set

This turn is often used on a wide, open slope and can be done at any speed, including high speed. The only place where it should not be tried is on an extremely steep slope. However, for most slopes which are encountered in everyday skiing this turn can give you a lot of enjoyment.

1. From a traverse position the knees and hips are lowered and the pole is brought forward, ready to be planted.

6. Near the end of the turn the outside arm has completed circular motion, bringing the body square to the skis ready to start another turn.

2 & 3 With a light touch of the pole, the body is raised from the knees and hips. At this moment the skis are unweighted and become almost flat. As the skis are lightened, most of the weight is transferred to the outside ski. The uphill arm moves forward and to the outside as the skis begin turning slightly.

4 & 5. With a sudden downward motion of the knees, the skis continue to turn. During this downward motion, the body is in a slight *reverse position* (turned opposite to the direction of the turn; the same as counterrotation) at the same time that the outside arm moves forward. (Notice how the arms are held away from the body.)

Edge Set and Pole Action

If a skier wants to progress to the advanced stages of skiing, he must know how to make an edge set (*the platform at the beginning of the turn*). *Every good skier uses edge set before a turn in order to ski in control, particularly when skiing on a steep hill. I think that the ability to use it is the key to perfection in advanced skiing.*

It is as difficult to teach the edge set as it is to learn it, but it is well worth the effort once mastered, because from that point on, your

Start across the hill with the body square to the skis and with a slight knee bend. When a fair amount of momentum has been gained, release the edges and start the skis sliding downhill.

progress will be rapid. The greatest difficulty lies in synchronizing the pole plant with the firm downward motion and turning of the edges into the hill. All through the advanced-skiing section of this book, including the slalom instruction, notice how many times I use the edge set. Because of its importance I am showing you sequences from both the front and the rear. The following sequences show the first step and one of the easiest ways to learn proper edge set. Practice on a medium-grade slope with good snow conditions.

The lower arm and pole are brought forward in a circular motion. At the same time the knees are lowered and the tails of the skis are pushed downhill.

This is the critical moment of edge set. To stop the skis from sliding downhill, the downhill pole is planted and the knees are rolled into the hill causing the skis to edge. At the same time the whole body lowers into a semi-crouch position. Some weight is carried on both skis, although the downhill ski carries more than the uphill.

The skis are retracted and hopped back into a traverse line. This exercise should be repeated several times across a wide slope.

Edge Set Starting a Parallel Turn

Knees are well flexed and turned into the hill. Skis are edged and the downhill pole is planted.

The skis are retracted and hopped back uphill to a traverse line.

With a sudden downward motion of the knees, the tails of the skis are pushed out and the turn is started.

Edge Set and a Complete Parallel Turn

4. Notice the position of the hips in relation to the knees and how the outside arm is moving forward and to the outside.

1. The edges are set and the pole is planted. Note the position of the knees in relation to the upper body—this is angulation.

2. The body is raised and the skis are unweighted and hopped close to the fall line. The body is square to the skis upon landing, and most of the weight is carried on the outside ski.

3. With a sudden downward motion of the knees, the tails of the skis are pushed out and the turn continues.

Linked Sharp Turns with Edge Set

Making a sharp turn with edge set requires more knee action and a more powerful throw of the outside arm at the beginning of the turn. A firm pole plant is extremely important because the pole acts as a strong pivot point for the sharp turn. At the beginning of the turn, notice the turning action of the upper body in relation to the position of the hips. When the skis are crossing the fall line, notice how the body changes its position. Then, when the skis start crossing the fall line into the new direction, the knees and the skier's control of his edges contribute a great deal to the sharpness of the turn. To get some idea of the sharpness of the turn, study how much my skis have come across the fall line at the end of the turn. This type of turn is used very often on steep hills.

At the end of one turn the edges are set and the pole is ready to be planted.

With an upward motion and a powerful forward thrust with the outside arm, the skis are unweighted and begin to turn.

As the skis enter the fall line, note the almost square position of the body and how much the skis are edged.

The forward knee pressure is increased, and the tails of the skis are pushed out. The outside pole is moving forward. The skis move well across the fall line and I am ready to set the edges and plant the pole for the next turn.

Narrow Edge-Set Turns

This is the same sequence in a narrow corridor of slalom flags set approximately nine feet apart. I am using this illustration of sharp turns with strong edge set to point out that a narrow trail can be skied in control with parallel turns. Skiing between poles is very good practice for anyone who is hesitant about skiing narrow, wooded trails.

Edge Set on a Very Steep Hill

This is similar to the preceding sequence except that now I am demonstrating on a much steeper hill. To minimize your speed on a steep slope, the edge set must be stronger and more pronounced and the angulation of your body must be increased.

The edges of the skis are strongly set at the moment the downhill pole is planted. Notice how the body is extremely angulated and how the downhill arm is low and held away from the body to allow for the steepness of the slope.

With a powerful upward motion, the tails of the skis are unweighted and moved close to the fall line.

As the skis come in contact with the snow, the knee action is greatly increased and the body moves forward. The outside arm moves forward and the pole is ready to be planted for the next turn.

Edge Set Using Both Poles on an Extremely Steep Slope

These photographs were taken on a slope of approximately 55 to 57 degrees. This is about as steep a hill as you can turn on properly. Both poles are used as an aid in pivoting the skis and in maintaining balance.

During the edge set, notice the position of both poles and arms and how my upper body is facing directly downhill.

With the tips of the skis on the snow, the tails are lifted slightly and placed close to the fall line. A powerful knee push is important. Because of the steepness of the slope, my arms are carried high to keep the tips of the poles from hitting the snow. The body is well forward.

Jump Christie

Jump christies are commonly used by top skiers, although sometimes unconsciously. This type of turn is useful to clear one or more bumps, or to jump over a large bump and make a turn on the other side of it. Jump christies can sometimes be used to advantage in difficult snow such as breakable crust, wind-blown crust, or soft, spring conditions. This turn is very similar to any round parallel turn, except that both skis are jumped a considerable distance when unweighted. The length of the jump depends upon the terrain, but at first you should try jumping only a few feet, as in the following sequence.

1. The body is lowered from the hips and knees and the pole is planted.

4. As the sharpness of the turn increases, notice the increased edging of the skis and the angulated position of the body. Most of the weight is on the outside ski, although there is some on the inside ski as well. At the end of the turn, the body comes square to the skis.

2. The body is raised and the skis are jumped off the snow and turned slightly. While the skis are in the air, the body is square to the skis and both arms are extended to the sides for balance.

3. When the skis come in contact with the snow, the shock is absorbed by a lowering of the knees. With a slight edging of the skis, a lowering of the knees, and a forward circular movement of the outside arm, the skis continue to turn.

Jump Christie in Deep Snow

This is a bit more advanced than the jump christie shown in the preceding sequence of pictures. You will notice that I am in the air longer and cover more distance in the air. Upon landing, my body seems to be almost exaggerated in its low crouch position in order to absorb the shock and to keep from sinking too deep into the snow.

The body is lowered and the pole is planted in preparation for the jump.

The skis are jumped and turned while in the air. The outside arm and pole are moving forward.

When the skis come in contact with the snow the body is lowered into a semi-crouch position to absorb shock and the pole is ready to be planted in preparation for the next jump. In a jump christie in deep snow the weight should be carried evenly on both skis as much as possible.

Parallel Turns in Deep Snow

The three sets of pictures that follow show a sharp round turn with edge set, a medium-sharp turn with edge set, and a fall-line turn without edge set. Notice the difference in the tracks in the powder snow.

SHARP ROUND TURNS WITH LITTLE EDGE SET

In picture 3 notice that my skis are almost across the fall line and that the edges are being set. In picture 4 notice the angle and position of the pole plant and how the skis come to the top of the snow when unweighted.

Parallel Turns in Deep Snow (continued)

MEDIUM ROUND TURNS WITH LITTLE EDGE SET

This turn is not as sharp as that in the previous sequence. The arm is straighter and the position of the pole plant is a bit more forward. The up-and-down motion is not quite as pronounced.

Parallel Turns in Deep Snow (continued)

FALL-LINE SKIING WITHOUT EDGE SET

Since the turn is held closer to the fall line the down-and-up motion is even less pronounced and the forward movement of the arm is less forceful.

JUMPING AND TRICK SKIING

Riding Small, Sharp Bumps

It is usually possible when riding small, sharp bumps to keep the skis in contact with the snow at all times. However, if the hollow is very sharp this is sometimes impossible and the skis may become slightly airborne.

Coming out of a hollow to the top of a bump, the body is raised.

When the skis are about to go over the bump, the knees are pushed forward and the body is lowered.

On the downhill side of the bump the body is in a low position. ⟶

Riding Small, Sharp Bumps (continued)

Riding over the next bump the hollow is short and my skis have become slightly airborne.

The body is almost entirely erect before landing in preparation for absorbing the shock when landing in the next hollow.

Upon landing, the body sinks to a crouch position to absorb the shock and the arms are brought forward for balance.

Prejumping Small Bumps

Here the skis are jumped off the snow and lifted over the bump to land on the downhill side.

Approaching the bump, the body is in a semi-crouch position with both arms held forward.

The skis are jumped before the bump and the arms and body are lowered. As the skis are crossing the bump, the tips are dropped and the body moves forward.

On the downhill side of the bump the body rises slightly to prepare to absorb shock.

Prejumping a Small Bump and Jumping a Large Bump

Sometimes when skiing you may come to a small bump, a deep hollow, and then a larger bump. The small bump may be prejumped as described on the previous pages, but if the hollow is very deep and the next bump large, you may not have the time to prejump again. In this case you will become airborne over the second bump. If this happens remember to hold a proper tuck position in the air.

Upon landing after prejumping the small bump, and before reaching the next, larger bump, my body rises slightly to prepare for the jump.

When the skis become airborne, the knees are tucked up close to the chest and the tips are dropped slightly. The arms are well forward and low.

Before landing, the body rises and is ready to absorb the shock of the landing.

Jumping a Series of Bumps

When skiing at reasonably high speed it is sometimes necessary to jump a number of bumps. This takes good judgment in knowing how far to jump. It is also extremely important to keep a proper body position while in the air.

As the skier approaches a large, sharp bump, the body is in a semi-crouch position with arms well forward.

As the skis become airborne, the knees are drawn up close to the upper body.

The arms are extended completely to the front to help balance, and the tips of the skis become parallel to the ground. ⟶

Jumping a Series of Bumps (continued)

When the skier crosses the last bump, the knees are lowered and the tips of the skis are dropped to follow the contour of the bump.

Before the landing, the arms and body rise to prepare to absorb the shock.

Upon landing, the skier lowers his body into a semi-crouch position to absorb the shock.

Airplane Turn

An airplane turn is a jump from a medium or large bump with a change of direction while in the air. This is often used when jumping from one mogul to the downhill side of another. The approach to the bump is the same as in the preceding sequences. On a hill with lots of moguls it is possible to make a series of these airplane turns.

The skis are lifted and become airborne.

While the skis are airborne they are turned to the desired direction.

The body extends and prepares to absorb shock upon landing.

Upon landing, the skier lowers his body to absorb shock. Notice that the left pole has moved forward during the descent to be ready to plant for the next jump in the opposite direction.

Jump Turn with Both Poles

A jump turn is a quick means of changing direction in any kind of snow. It is often used by expert skiers.

The edges of the skis are set and both poles are planted.

With a sudden jump, the skis are turned around the inside pole into the new direction.

The skis are airborne and almost completely turned in the new direction. The right, or outside, pole is lifted and brought around with the skis.

When the skis return to the snow in the new direction, the knees flex to absorb shock and the poles are held to either side for balance.

Geländesprung, or Double Pole-Jump Turn

This is a quick means of turning around that can be fun to do on the edge of a bump or the top of a steep hill. It takes a fair amount of strength in the arms.

With your hands on top of the poles and all of your weight carried by your arms, the tails of the skis are kicked out and up and turned. The skis return to the snow in the opposite direction.

113

360-Degree Turnaround from a Stop Christie

This is an interesting trick for experts, which should be done on a gradual hill or over a sharp knoll.

The turnaround starts from a sharp stop christie with the body in an extreme forward crouch position.

From the stop christie, the body is quickly extended and the skis are jumped and turned uphill.

The upper body jackknifes to drop the tips of the skis.

The skis have turned a complete 360 degrees and land in the fall line.

One-Ski Skiing

This is good practice for balance and edge control. It is also fun, and challenging. It can be done with a single pole or with both poles, but I recommend using both in the beginning to maintain balance. The mechanics of one-ski skiing are exactly the same as those of skiing on two skis: the preparation for the turn is the same, the unweighting is the same, and the turn itself is the same. You will find it easier at first if you jump the skis off the ground with a fair amount of support from your poles. Later on you may use one pole and unweight the ski without so much lift.

Lower the body and plant both poles.

With much of the weight supported by the poles, the ski is jumped and landed close to the fall line.

Upon landing it is important that the body leans well forward to keep balance.

At the end of the turn the body lowers in preparation for the next turn.

COMPETITIVE SKIING

Skate Turn with Tip Pull

This is a very advanced maneuver. It is much used in competition skiing, especially in slalom and giant slalom, to gain height in a turn and to accelerate off the uphill ski. It may be done with one pole but most racers use both. It is very important to be in good physical and skiing condition when attempting this type of turn. There are two variations of the skate turn. One is done with aid of tip pull (*a tilted inside ski*) *and the other without.*

2. Near the end of the turn the skis are split into a slight "V" and the uphill ski is advanced. At this point most of the weight is carried on the edge of the advanced ski. Simultaneously both poles are moved forward, ready to be planted.

3. The weight is carried entirely on the uphill ski while both poles are being planted. The upper body is turning and beginning to face downhill. With a thrust of the poles the inside ski is lifted.

1. Here I am in the first half of a high-speed parallel turn. Notice the hip position in relation to the upper body.

4. The outside ski is changed onto its inside edge. At this moment the tip of the inside ski is tilted and pressed against the snow to produce tip pull. The tilting of this ski on the snow will increase and quicken the turning power.

5. As the turn continues the inside ski is placed parallel to the outside ski as in any other turn. Notice the position of the arms and that the body is square over the skis.

Skate Turn Without Tip Pull

This is exactly the same as the preceding turn except that in picture 4 my skis are brought together without tip pull. This type of skate turn is most useful when you do not need to make an extremely sharp turn after the skate step. Picture 3 shows how much the uphill ski advances and how the upper body lunges forward when both poles are brought to the front for pole planting.

3.

4.

1.

2.

5.

6.

Slalom

Slalom racing is a challenge for any good skier because it is the ultimate test of a skier's proficiency. Maneuvering through various combinations of gates is also excellent practice for any skier who wishes to perfect his technique and timing. The secret of slalom racing is to hold the shortest and fastest line from gate to gate, regulating your speed so that an even pace is maintained throughout the entire course. Sometimes it is necessary to check your speed in order to take certain combinations rhythmically. Most of these checks are accomplished by the edge set, which was covered in the section on advanced skiing. While running slalom the skis are kept parallel as much as possible, except when you split your skis to use a skate step.

On the following pages there are picture sequences showing how to take various slalom gate combinations. To give you a graphic idea of how these gates appear on the hill, there are illustrations of the combinations used in the instruction and several other combinations.

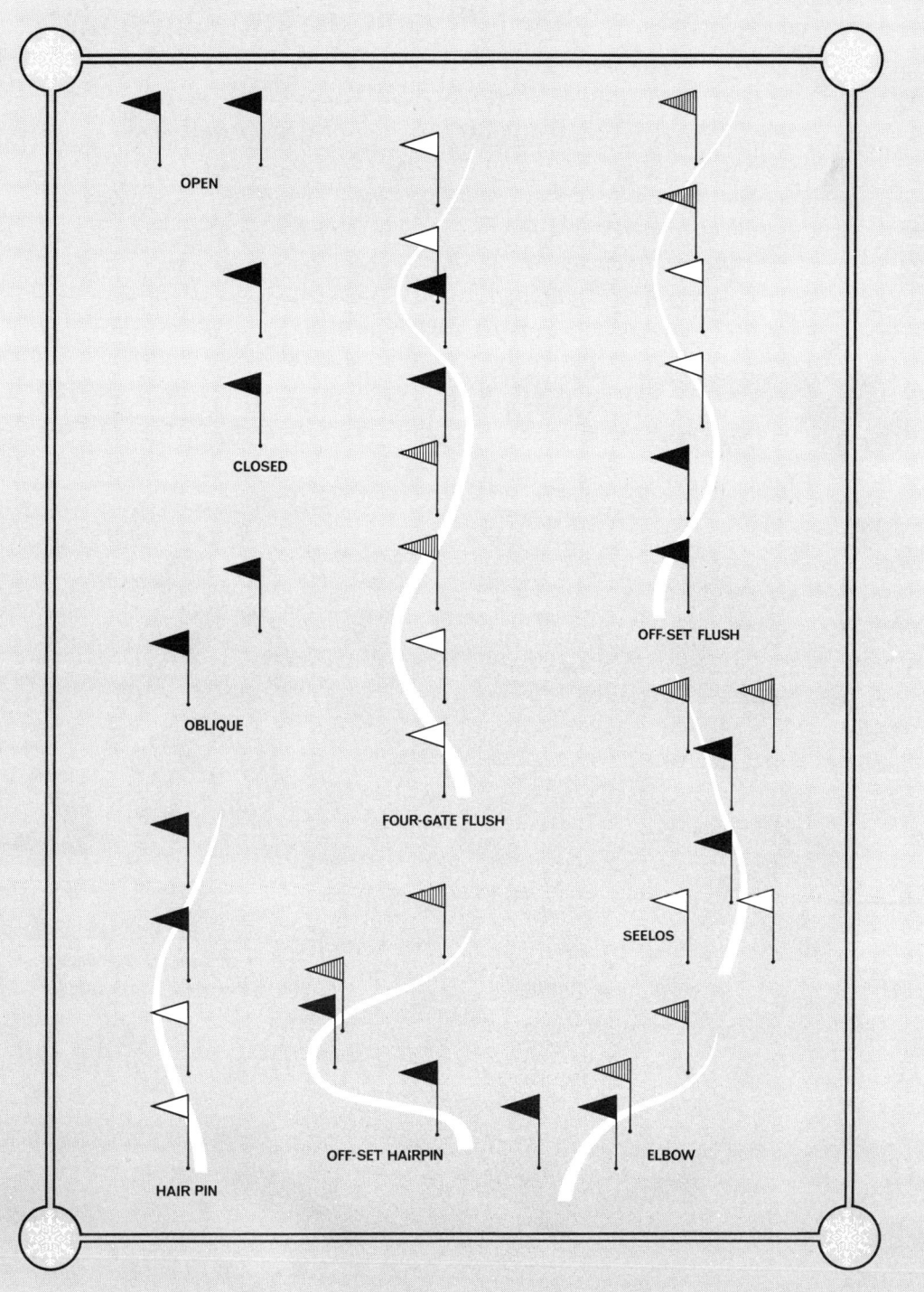

Side-Hill Hairpin and Open Gate

A closed gate is made up of one set of flags, one flag above the other, usually so placed that the entrance to the gate is not visible upon approach. The entrance of an open gate is always visible upon approach. A hairpin is made up of two closed gates, one set directly above the other. This sequence shows a hairpin set diagonally across the fall line followed by an open gate. It can be a very difficult combination when set on an icy surface. I have always found it best to enter a hairpin high, close to the upper flag.

The hairpin is entered from the high side in a parallel turn.

In the middle of the hairpin the skate step is executed.

The weight is transferred to the uphill ski and the downhill ski is stepped parallel. Notice the projection of the arm. This allows the skier to use the pole to push off.

The skis are now parallel and turning around the open gate. The inside shoulder leads to allow me to get closer to the gate.

Four Closed Gates

In this sequence I am using a parallel turn and a modified skate step. There is one thing here that I would like to point out because it has been misunderstood by many people, including racers. You will notice that any time my body is in a reverse position I am hugging a gate. As soon as my body has passed the gate I quickly transfer my weight and move out of this position. The position I adopt in picture 3 is only held for a split second. Some people make the mistake of trying to hold the reverse position throughout the whole turn, resulting in putting too much weight on the inside ski for too long a time, which causes overedging and leaning into the hill. Overedging, of course, slows you down.

The gate is entered in a parallel turn. The skis begin to split slightly and the weight is carried on the uphill ski.

The downhill ski is picked up and brought parallel to the uphill ski, and the outside arm is projected forward. ⟶

Four Closed Gates (continued)

As I enter the next gate, notice the inside shoulder leading and the positioning of the hips in relation to the upper body. This is a good example of angulation.

As my feet pass the gate the weight is transferred to the uphill ski.

The downhill ski is picked up and stepped parallel.

Notice how close my body is to the pole in the last gate and how it is again reversed, or angulated.

Closed Off-Set Gates: Comparison Runs

On the following pages you will find the same run demonstrated by me, Pepi Stiegler, and Adrien Duvillard. The three individual slalom runs were taken from the same place with a sequence camera. If you compare the pictures you will find that much the same technique is used by all three of us. Notice how we all use the skate step in certain places in the course and how our pole action and body angulation are almost identical, though our racing careers stem from three different origins: Canada, Austria, and France.

Ernie McCulloch's Run

Pepi Stiegler's Run

Adrien Duvillard's Run

McCulloch

Stiegler

Duvillard

134

McCulloch

Stiegler

Duvillard

Straight Flush

This is a sequence of the three of us skiing a four-gate straight flush set side by side. Notice the similarity of the body positioning, the pole action, and the knee action. Adrien is on the left and Pepi on the right.

Straight Flush (continued)

140

Straight Flush: Comparison Runs

These two pictures show a straight flush with the three of us skiing in single file. Again, note how the poles, hands, and feet show remarkable similarity.

Giant Slalom

The difference between giant slalom and slalom is that giant slalom gates are farther apart, making a much faster course, and usually only closed and open gates are used. It is also longer and covers more difficult terrain. A giant slalom is similar to a tightly controlled downhill course.

The important thing to remember when skiing a giant slalom is to regulate your speed so that you are high in all the gates and not caught low in some of the more difficult combinations.

This picture shows me entering an open giant-slalom gate.

Downhill Crouches

There are two basic crouches used in downhill. One is a very low crouch for the greatest speed. The other is similar except that the body is a little higher to allow more knee action and better balance over rough terrain. It might also be used in a long race to rest your legs for a second or two.

This is the low crouch, which is often called the egg position. Two sections of my body, from the hips to the shoulders and from the hips to the knees, are both almost parallel to my skis. My hands are together and my poles are tucked under my arms.

This stance is similar but my hips are carried somewhat higher.